Exposing
The Spirit of Anger

APOSTLE STEPHEN A. GARNER

RIVERS PUBLISHING COMPANY
CHICAGO, ILLINOIS

All materials are original works by:
Stephen A. Garner
Cover Design by Giant Killers Media Design

Rivers Publishing Company
Stephen A. Garner Ministries
P.O. Box 1545, Bolingbrook, IL 60440
E-mail: sagarnerministries@gmail.com
www.sagministries.com

Second Printing 2010

Unless otherwise indicated, all scriptural quotations are taken from the King James Version of the Holy Bible. All Hebraic and Greek definitions are taken the Strong's Exhaustive Concordance, Baker Book House: Grand Rapids, Michigan

ISBN 978-0-9844783-2-3

Printed in the United States of America

TABLE OF CONTENTS

FOREWORD

There are countless numbers of people who are overwhelmed with the cares of life in our ever-changing society. These cares, if left unmet, often lead to fierce manifestations of anger. The end results usually cause much more damage than intended; and for some, resulting in situations they wished had never occurred.

This book is written to serve as a tool for uncovering hell's strategies through the use of the spirit of anger. You will learn the progressive and destructive courses of anger and specific demonic powers that support it. My prayer is that as God exposes its works in your life, He will also impart unto you the grace needed to help you defeat this vicious spirit.

Demons hate exposure. The light of God's Word does just that and thereby gives us insight and revelation on how to triumph over our enemies. I endeavor to bring as much light to the destructive spirits of anger, wrath, and malice so that the stronghold they have in your life or those you are praying for can be broken. Jesus says in John 3:19b, "...men loved darkness rather than light because their deeds were evil." The gospel of Jesus Christ is the glorious light that enlightens the hearts of men and brings salvation (deliverance). Therefore, demons despise light and illumination; and are defeated when the Light of Truth comes.

CHAPTER 1

THE ANATOMY OF ANGER

There is an evil spirit at work that is imposing itself upon the inhabitants of the earth today. This spirit possesses the potential to cause much havoc, devastation, and misery; if it is allowed to manifest and flourish. His name is ANGER. The scriptures depict various situations where God Himself got angry. His consistent anger with the wicked is revealed in Psalms 7:11 "God is a righteous judge, Yea, a God that hath indignation every day."

The Word of God depicts His continual anger and hostility toward the acts of the wicked is felt on a daily basis. It is not a sin to become angry for righteousness' sake. However, it is more often than not that when we become angry, it is not because we are demonstrating the righteousness of God to punish wickedness. On the contrary, we usually manifest anger because we perceive a personal injustice is being done to us. Can you picture a raging bull, with the fury of hell blowing out of his nostrils, about to be released from a stall, with a helpless cowboy on his back who is determined to break him? Regardless of the cowboy's skill, this is an impossible task. This picture exemplifies the lives of many people, especially believers who are driven by the spirit of anger. When the enemy is successful in overwhelming us with anger, we become just as that raging bull; and our families and loved ones are like helpless cowboys trying to tame a ferocious bull. The Bible says in Proverbs 16:32, "He that is slow to anger is better than the mighty; and he that ruleth his spirit than he that taketh a city." The fruit of temperance in Galatians 5 helps us to become a greater force than the mighty and as we exercise discipline, it will give us the fortitude of one who can take a city.

The Hebraic term for anger, aph, (#639) is defined as that of rapid breathing in passion, a dilating of the nostrils and breathing that becomes more difficult. The word, anger, in the Greek (#3709) is described as a desire as reaching forth or excitement of the mind i.e. (by anal.) violent passion (by impl.) punishment, anger, indignation, vengeance. Often, when we experience seasons of stress, pressure, tension or situations of urgency; we reach a boiling point. It is difficult to stay sober and alert when we have these encounters, when it is easy to be used of the devil by the spirit of anger. From prison cells to bitter divorces, many have become victims of anger's anatomy. There are many people bound in tragic situations today because they yielded to the spirit of anger. They are tormented by shame and even guilt. The world offers us alternative courses to manage anger and get in touch with our inner self. Yet, what we truly need is deliverance and a revelation of when anger leads to sin. Therefore, it is demonic. Deliverance is what we need; not anger management.

Genesis 4 provides the most thorough account of how destructive the spirit of anger can become in a person's life. In this passage, Cain and Abel both brought their sacrificial offering before the Lord, but He accepted Abel's offering and rejected Cain's. Some may ask the question: Why was Abel's offering accepted and Cain's offering rejected? God cursed the ground because of Adam's sin, according to Genesis 3:17. Cain presented the fruit of a cursed source (the ground) by God, which made his offering unacceptable. On the other hand, Abel offered God a living sacrifice that pleased Him. Adam had failed to instruct Cain on what type of offering would please God. Cain even chose an occupation of working the land that was cursed. He received the full blunt of his parents' cursed inheritance and punishment by being the firstborn of a couple who were rejected by God. From this passage, we see why Cain had become susceptible to the devil and manifested unrestrained anger that ultimately led him to murder his brother. I believe there was a network of spirits already at work in Cain because of what was passed on through his bloodline, according to Exodus 20:5. Even Abel was not free from the sin of his parents; just because he was cut off prematurely. I believe his untimely death was a direct result of his parents' inherited sinful legacy. The devil does not care who opens the door for him to come in.

His primary concern is just to get in and cause destruction as we see with the first family.

"And the LORD said unto Cain, Why art thou wroth? and why is thy countenance fallen?" Genesis 4:6

In this verse, the Spirit of God reveals strategies in how to overcome the wicked purposes of anger induced by demons. God asked Cain a twofold question, Why are you wroth? The term, *wroth*, means to blaze up, to become hot, to burn, to be displeased and become jealous. He also asked the question: Why has your countenance fallen? God understood that anger affects our facial features, because it rises to the forehead; as mentioned in the Hebraic definition. When we stop to ask ourselves: Why we are blazing and take a look at our actions, we can then receive the grace to escape the condemnation of the devil. Cain's countenance had fallen because he gave into the devil's plan through his anger. The countenance and appearance of many have also fallen within the Body of Christ. Spirits of disgrace, dishonor, guilt, condemnation and a host of other demonic cohorts have invaded many and become their lot in life; rather than receiving the benefits of God's mercy, grace, wisdom and righteousness. People today are being punished because they have allowed the spirit of anger, with its unwarranted passions, to lead them down a path of destruction.

"If thou doest well, shalt thou not be accepted? And if thou doest not well, sin lieth at the door. And unto thee shall be his desire, and thou shalt rule over him."

Genesis 4:7

Doing what is right in the sight of God will definitely assure God's approval and favor upon our lives. The issue of God's rejection has everything to do with sin. God told Cain that if he failed to do well, sin would be at his door. It was sin's strong desire that wanted to rule over him, but God's instruction encouraged Cain to rule over them. Notice how God refers to sin as an actual personality by describing it as "him." This portrayal depicts how sin opens the door for demons to enter our lives. Genesis 4:7 in The New English Translation reads, If you do well, you are accepted: if not, sin is a demon crouching at the door. It shall be eager for you, and will be mastered by it. Genesis 4:7 in The Jerusalem Translation also reads, If you are well-disposed ought you not to lift up your head? But if you are ill-disposed, is it not sin at the door like a crouching beast hungering for you, which you must master. In these scripture translations, we can see a clearer connection with sin and demonic activity. It is difficult to separate sin from demons. I am not saying that if you sin, you automatically have demons come into your life. However, if one continues to practice sin, you can rest assured that demonic spirits will come in to compensate you for your wrongdoing before God. They are crouching beasts, hungering for those who chose to remain immoral.

Cain lived a life of utter ruin. The demon of anger opened him to a life of much despair and hardship. He was cursed from the earth. Spirits of poverty, paranoia, suspicion, confusion, wandering, barrenness, condemnation, fear, and restlessness became the tormentors of Cain's life as described in Genesis 4:11-14.

"A soft answer turneth away wrath: but GRIEVOUS WORDS STIR UP ANGER".

Proverbs 15:1

Words are powerful and carry supernatural abilities to restore, heal, and deliver. Jesus said in John 6:63b, "The words I speak to you they are spirit and they are life." Likewise, the devil will stir up the spirit of anger in our lives through speaking heinous and shameful words. Our hearts are the source for our words. If we hide God's Word in our heart, then His Word is what we will speak and it will spare us from unnecessary attacks. Demonic spirits attach themselves to our words. Therefore, we must avoid evil communication, for it corrupts good manners.

"Ye have heard that it was said by them of old time, thou shalt not kill; and whosoever shall kill shall be in danger of the judgment, but I say unto you, that whosoever is angry with his brother without a cause shall be in danger of judgment: and whosoever shall say to his brother, RACA, shall be in danger of the council: but whosoever shall say, thou FOOL, shall be in danger of hell fire."

Matthew 5:21-22

Jesus revealed the spiritual meaning behind the sixth commandment in Exodus 20:13, "Thou shalt not kill." Notice how anger is the spirit at work that has a course set for hell fire. The Lord teaches that if we are angry at our brother without a cause, we are in danger of judgment. This action was equated with actually killing your brother; in the eyes of Jesus. He then continues to show how scornful words will cause even greater harm. The Greek term, *raca* is used and it literally means worthless and empty. For believers to use this kind of language against another is to demonize God's creation. It is rooted in pride. The Bible states in Proverbs 16:18, "Pride goes before destruction and a haughty spirit before a fall." The anger that fills our hearts with harshness will ultimately lead to wickedness. Jesus said this will put one in danger of the council. The last terminology the Lord uses is fool, defined as a dull or stupid person, which is literally spiteful in nature. It is rooted in hatred and utter disgust. The Lord says this will put you in danger of hell fire. Hell fire comes from the Greek word geenna (gheh'-en-nah #1067) which is a place of everlasting punishment. There are eternal consequences when we choose not to seek and get deliverance from anger. We become unfit for kingdom service and our sacrificial offerings of time, service, worship, and prayer before God is literally unacceptable.

"...whoso provoketh him to anger sinneth against his own soul."

Proverbs 20:2

The Word warns believers of the dangers of provoking God and one another. Believers are told why we should not provoke God and parents are encouraged not to provoke their children. When we provoke each other to anger, we sin against our own souls. An American Translation reads "... he who provokes him to anger forfeits his life." To forfeit means to relinquish, hand over or give up. I believe that many relationships, especially covenant relationships, have been aborted or altogether destroyed due to the pressures that come from spirits assigned against us. In many instances, you will find that the spirit of anger is usually dominant and at work.

"It is better to dwell in the wilderness, than with a contentious and an angry woman."

Proverbs 21:19

There is more peace found in being a drifter, one who has no place of stability, than with a brawling, bitter-tongued, and angry woman. The key revealed here is that we should avoid people who have reached a boiling point; totally engulfed with anger.

"Make no friendship with an angry man; and with a furious man thou shalt not go: Lest thou learn his ways and get a snare to thy soul."

Proverbs 22:24-25

Covenant relationships are important and necessary in life. Throughout scripture, we see where God consistently warns His people about the nations that they were not to have relationships with. The children of Israel were reproved about connecting and intermingling with surrounding nations because they would turn them away from following God. These nations would ultimately lead them to idolatry; which would cause God's judgment to come upon them as written in Deuteronomy 7:1-4. Those whom we have fellowship with will influence us in one way or another; simply because of the relationship. Angry and furious people will steer the righteous into paths of wickedness and bondage. The devil sets traps for the righteous and those whom we come into fellowship with can become a pawn in the devil's hand to ensnare us; especially the angry. The end result will be captivity in the soul.

"An angry man stirreth up strife, and a furious man aboundeth in transgression. A man's pride will bring him low but honor shall uphold the humble in spirit."

Proverbs 29:22-23

Envy, strife and confusion tend to every evil work. In this passage, we see the spirit of anger found right at the root of strife. Many believers embrace this spirit and it has destroyed many churches and ministries. The word, strife, means to be in conflict, discord, friction and hostility. When we fail to address the root causes, we often create bigger problems. Demons will and have always played on the ignorance of the saints. They hate being discerned, exposed, and driven out of their hiding places within the life of a believer. The increase of lawlessness in the land is a result of individuals operating in greater degrees of anger and fury. Pride, haughtiness, arrogance, cockiness, vanity and egotism are all cohorts of anger. Angry people manifest strong spirits of pride and vanity. It is difficult to converse with them and ever see eye to eye on anything because they have exalted themselves. To disagree with them will most definitely guarantee confrontation of the worst kind. Many businesses, marriages, friendships, personal health and other valuable and significant things have been destroyed because of anger and pride. Prideful people will not humble themselves and angry people refuse to be humbled. Isaiah 5:14-16 reads,

"Therefore hell hath enlarged herself, and opened her mouth without measure: and their glory, and their multitude, and their pomp, and he that rejoiceth, shall descend into it. And the mean man shall be brought down, and the mighty man shall be humbled, and the eyes of the lofty shall be humbled: But the LORD of hosts shall be exalted in judgment, and God that is holy shall be sanctified in righteousness."

"For where envying and strife is, there is confusion and every evil work."

James 3:16

Many of the evils of the past and those atrocities being committed today were birthed out of strife. The countless conflicts and struggles in the earth today can be found rooted in wrath; which leads to some form of strife. The key to individuals, cities, regions, and nations being freed from wrath that are accredited to strife, is in the redemptive work of the shedding of Christ's blood. Apostle Paul declares in Romans 5:8-9, "But God commendeth His love toward us, in that, while we were yet sinners, Christ died for us. Much more than, being now justified by his blood, we shall be saved from WRATH through him."

The wrath of man worketh not the righteousness of God. Wherefore lay apart all filthiness and superfluity of naughtiness, and receive with meekness the engrafted word, of which is able to save your soul."

James 1:20-21

Unrighteousness is the final resting place for those who continue to yield to the spirit of anger. Regardless of how one may try to please God; when anger is raging inside them, something will always set them off and destruction will not be far behind. Solomon declares in Ecclesiastes 7:9, "Anger rest in the bosom of fools." When anger takes root in us, foolishness is sure to follow. Harshness, bitter words, and destructive behaviors, which are inclined to hell itself, are commonly produced. Immorality, naughtiness, filthiness and a nest of other demonic works are found rooted in anger.

CHAPTER II

WRATH: AN AGENT OF VIOLENCE

"Therefore rejoice, ye heavens, and ye that dwell in them. Woe to the inhabitants of the earth and of the sea! For the devil is come down unto you having GREAT WRATH, because he knoweth that he hath but a short time."

Revelation 12:12

Revelations 12 gives us a prophetic picture of the Church (The Woman with Child) and the devil (great red dragon) as warring wonders in the heavens. There is angelic involvement in this battle that results in the devil being thrust out of Heaven. The heavens rejoice in victory, but there is a grievous judgment of WOE pronounced on the inhabitants of the earth and the sea. The fiery red dragon that made war with the Church (The Woman) has been cast out of Heaven and is now released upon the earth with great or mega wrath. He is now making war with the Saints and is burning with indignation. The word, *wrath*, comes from the Greek word *thumos* (#2372) which means passion; as if breathing hard, fierceness, indignation. It is also defined as an outburst of the state of one's mind. *Thuo* (#2380) is another Greek term used to define wrath. It means to rush at, breath hard, blow smoke, to make a sacrifice, to immolate, to slaughter for any purpose, to kill; to slay. This describes a fire breathing dragon resembling the one described in Revelations 12.

Because of the spirit of wrath, the earth is filled with violence and other acts of ungodliness. I believe this is because we have failed to identify and study our real enemy; the devil. He is a worthy adversary that has inflicted much injustice and wickedness upon the Church and earth. Unlike anger, yet demonically connected; the spirit of wrath is found to impact territories through a principality or a ruling spirit in a region. John refers to the earth and the sea as recipients of the devil's fury as he pronounces his grievous woe. The implications behind the manifestations of the spirit of wrath produce territorial effects.

"Scornful men bring a city into a snare: but wise men turn away WRATH."

Proverbs 29:8

Destructive demonstrations with cities and regions are born through the hearts and actions of scornful people. When one ethnic group, nation, or class of people display scorn or rejects another, then the door for the spirit of wrath is opened. From the most populated regions of the world to the most remote, I believe the spirit of wrath is found at the root of racism and other social ills that keep people divided. The intense hatred of the devil for humanity has expressed itself without restraint through the spirit of wrath; thus devastating entire communities, cities and even nations. Places where you find continual hostilities among ethnic groups or nations rising against nations, gives clear evidence of the existence and work of WRATH as a RULING spirit. This serves as another example of the impact the devil has had on our society throughout the ages through this spirit.

"For we wrestle not against flesh and blood, but against principalities, against powers, against the rulers of the darkness of this world, against spiritual wickedness in high places."

Ephesians 6:12.

"A man of great wrath shall suffer punishment: for if thou deliver him, yet thou must do it again."

Proverbs 19:19

The spirit of wrath is an inflictor of suffering and punishment. People who are bound by this spirit can easily be perceived as victims. However, in the book of Proverbs, they are viewed as tyrants; because they are the perpetrators stuck in a never-ending destructive cycle. The American Standard Translation reads: A man of great wrath shall bear the penalty; for if thou deliver him, thou must do it yet again. The Basic English

Translation states; A man of great wrath will have to take his punishment: for if you get him out of trouble you will have to do it again. Whatever the case, there is a need for consistent deliverance. Because they lack self control, these individuals need help from those who are neutral in the situation that may place them in the line of punishment. Short-fused is a good term to describe them. The moment they feel threatened, they just lose it. Yet, once the dust settles and the smoke clears, the help of another is required. They may need bond money, a hospital payment and legal assistance; just to name a few.

"For jealousy is the rage of a man: therefore he will not spare in the day of vengeance."

Proverbs 6:34

Jealousy, envy, and covetousness are demons that must be dealt with when confronting the spirit of wrath. They help to stir him up. The Berkeley Translation reiterates, "For jealousy rouses a strongman's anger; in the day of vengeance he will not spare." Proverbs 27:4 declares, "Wrath is cruel, and anger is outrageous; but who can stand before envy?" Jealousy and envy will cause one to faint and even destroy their own fruitfulness. Frustration, fruitlessness and impatience can sometimes also lead to a blow up. This is especially present with those in leadership, when no increase is seen from genuine efforts put forth to advance the Kingdom. It is during these times, we can become most vulnerable and susceptible to the attacks of the devil. Galatians 6:9 exhorts believers "… not be weary in well doing for we shall reap if we faint not."

"He will not regard any ransom; neither will he rest content, though thou givest many gifts."

Proverbs 6:35

There is a manifestation of ruthlessness and a tendency to be merciless among individuals who are bound by wrath. The Lamsa Translation reads; "He will not regard any ransom: nor will he listen, though you increase the bribe." When an individual is manifesting in the spirit of wrath; no amount of gifts, ransoms, or any kind of compensation can satisfy him. This measure of wrath should only be reserved for the devil himself. Yet, we have found this behavior to be prevalent among the saints; in the way we treat one other. I believe humility is the strongest countermeasure when dealing with this spirit. The Wisdom of God is needed to release the grace to overcome and turn wrath away.

"If thou hast done foolishly in lifting up thyself, or if thou hast thought evil, lay thine hand upon thy mouth. Surely the churning of milk bringeth forth butter, and the wringing of the nose bringeth forth blood: so the forcing of WRATH bringeth forth STRIFE."

Proverbs 30:32-33

Pride, self promotion, haughtiness, self-exaltation, and loftiness are spirits that will provoke the strongman of wrath to manifest. Many believers who struggle with selfishness usually manifest strong pride. Through selfishness and pride, the devil himself tried to take God's throne and rule. His words recorded in Isaiah 14:12-14 are rooted in selfishness with continual references to the word "I" (pride). The verses noted above instruct us to lay our hands on our mouths because our prideful words will definitely give way to wrath and cause strife. Most believers who struggle in the area of selfishness have spirits of wrath assigned to them. The moment something does not go their way (pride), harsh words and strife come forth because they are bound by wrath. The apparent outcome is similar to igniting flammable liquids or a fireworks display.

CHAPTER III

MALICE: A WEAPON OF MASS DESTRUCTION

Malice is defined as badness, depravity, malignity, naughtiness, wickedness and evil habits of the mind. As you can see, there is a progression of anger that leads to wrath and wrath that leads to malice. In the eyes of the legitimate legal system, those who are known as conspirators are viewed to be more dangerous to society than the individuals who actually commit a crime. The reason for this way of thinking is that those that conspire evil are able to get individuals or entire groups to carry out the wicked and cruel plans that come from thoughts harbored in their own evil imaginations. This depraved tendency is viewed as having too much influence or power over people. The law is designed to punish those whose influences can lead others to lawlessness. The hidden agenda of malice is rooted in moral wickedness. The devil has been very successful in infecting the entire planet with every kind of evil imagined to advance his kingdom. From those who join cults to governing officials. The kingdom of darkness has woven itself into every aspect of our societies.

"Wherefore lay apart all filthiness and superfluity of naughtiness, and receive with meekness the engrafted word, which is able to save your souls".

James 1:21

Moral wickedness is the culmination of anger when it reaches the stage of malice. The enemy knows that once we fail to abide by the truth of God's Word, then all restraints against him are removed. The New English Bible Translation reads, "Away then with all that sordid, and the MALICE that hurries to excess." The saints' failure to live in accordance with the Word will give way to malice and all the debauchery that comes along with it. Remember, the devil has come down to the earth having great wrath, according to Revelation 12:12. His objective is to drive us away from serving God and cause us to live our lives fulfilling the lusts of our flesh and imaginations. The earth seems to be set on a course of moral failure on every hand. Who would have ever imagined that we would be living in a day where even the marriage covenant between a man and woman would be questioned or challenged? Even in the eyes of some, this divine institution of covenant needs to be redefined. All tendencies are rooted in the wrath of the devil against mankind.

"...living in MALICE and envy, hateful, and hating one another."

Titus 3:3

The Word of God is clear on how we are to love one another. Jesus commands in Matthew 19:19, "Thou shalt love thy neighbor as thyself." The Lord then takes it a step further and instructs us to "Love our enemies, bless them that curse you, do good to them that hate you, and pray for them which despitefully use you, and persecute you; that you may be the children of your Father which is in heaven." Matthew 5:44-45a

Through the work of malice and hatred, the devil drives people to do just the opposite. He is in the business of soul winning as well. He understands that, if the kingdom of darkness is to prevail in the earth, he too needs sons and daughters. The devil is the destroyer and known as the father of lies. His kingdom is predicated upon lies, deception, pride, and hatred. Proverbs 10:18 states, "He that hideth hatred with lying lips, and he that slandereth is a fool." The reason why the spirit of malice is so dangerous is because it is usually concealed. This is the very nature of the devil. He hides himself and once his lie is received, destruction is at hand. This is how he interacted with Adam and Eve. With malicious intent in his heart for God's creation and subtlety upon his lips, he appeared a serpent and seduced them to rebel against God.

Since then, hatred has exponentially increased. When we conspire against each other, to promote envy and hatred out of corrupt living; the agenda of hell itself is enlarged. Disobedience, which is synonymous with rebellion, is at work among those who partake of such works. Ephesians 2:1-3 declares:

"And you hath he quickened, who were dead in trespasses and sins: Wherein in time past ye walked according to the course of this world, according to the prince of the power of the air, the spirit that now worketh in the children of disobedience: Among whom also we all had our conversation in times past in the lusts of our flesh, fulfilling the desires of the flesh and of the mind; and were by nature the children of wrath, even as others."

Apostle John warns Gaius concerning Diotrephes in III John. He was an unruly member seeking to gain preeminence among the brethren. Through accusation and self-promotion, he hindered the church from receiving the apostles in verses 9-10. Diotrephes had ridiculed the apostles with baseless talking and malicious words. Many believers who are enraged and fail to become delivered from anger will eventually become involved with some type of conspiracy within the church. The moment they are denied a platform, because of character flaws, they begin to start a church within the church. They have no problem conspiring against godly leaders in authority and even those who are in agreement with them. I believe, at the root of all church splits and division among the saints is the spirit of malice.

"But now ye also put off all these; anger, wrath, malice, blasphemy, filthy communication out of your mouth."

Colossians 3:8

We are admonished to put off anger, wrath and malice in sequential order. There is a connection to the operation of these spirits and the mouth. Proverbs 18:21 proclaims, "Death and life are in the power of the tongue: and they that love it shall eat the fruit thereof." Our words can become a powerful vehicle to release the works of darkness. Just as God spoke, "Let there be," and things came into existence. The plans of hell are given access into the earth by the vehicle of words. The spirit of anger excites the mind and is an intense expression of a passion and rage. The spirit of wrath releases the manifestations of anger. The spirit of malice orchestrates the connections of evil thoughts and their manifestations through our actions and conversation.

He that hateth dissembleth with his lips; and layeth up deceit within him: When he speaketh fair, believe him not: for there are seven abominations in his heart. Whose hatred is covered by deceit, his wickedness shall be shewed before the whole congregation."

Proverbs 26:24-26

There is an old adage that says, "Sticks and stones may break my bones, but words will never hurt me." This is the biggest lie ever told. More people have been destroyed through hate-inspired words than any battle fought. For ages, the devil has utilized dialogue that has produced death and destruction. Malice is at the root of hatred and it is a weapon of mass destruction. Entire nations, along with future generations, can be set upon a course of destruction by what has been given life through malicious conversations or words. We can rest assure that exposure of the works of this spirit can become a reality within the congregation of the righteous. Here is a powerful verse for every believer to continually pray found in Psalm 141:3: "Set a watch at my mouth and keep the door of my lips." This prayer will establish a safeguard to govern the words we speak and do not provide the devil with the ammunition needed to fuel his plans.

APPENDIX

TOOLS OF DELIVERANCE
Tactics to Rout Demons
(From Annihilating the Host of Hell by Win Worley)

<u>A Way for the Deliverance Worker To Get Started:</u>

1. Have a brief conversation about the reason the person is there for ministry.

2. General prayer and worship - focus on God and His glorious attributes.

3. Bind the powers over the area; break all assignments from the powers in the air to demons in the person. Ask for angelic protection (Hebrews 1:14).

4. Ask and receive by faith the gifts of the Spirit needed to minister.

<u>Governance During The Deliverance Session:</u>

1. Too many people commanding spirits (different ones) at the same time causes confusion for everyone; especially the person being ministered to.

2. Leadership of the session will often shift as the Holy Spirit directs.

3. Husbands are often the most effective in commanding spirits to leave their wives, with the support of others.

Tactics of Speaking to Demons:

1. Address the spirit by name and if he is not known, address by function.

   a. Either the Holy Spirit will give it, or
   b. The demon will reveal himself.
   c. Do not rely on either method exclusively - be open to the Holy Spirit in this area.

2. Repeatedly remind these spirits that your authority is given to you by Jesus Christ, "Who is far above all rule and authority." (Ephesians 1:21)

3. Remind them of their fate in Revelations 20:10 and other places in scripture (Job 30:3-8). Use the statement "The Lord Jesus Christ rebukes you" repeatedly, as a battering ram.

4. It is helpful to harass the demons to confess that Jesus Christ is their Lord.

5. Ruler demons often can be badgered for more information.

6. At times, you will command the ruler demon to go and clean out the lesser demons under him. If that does not work, reverse the tactics.

7. Bind and separate any interfering spirits as God leads.

8. There is no need to shout at demons since the battle is not in the flesh, but in the Spirit.

What To Expect In Receiving Deliverance

While many deliverances involve obvious physical manifestations, not all react in this manner. Some spirits leave quietly and non-violently. You may not have a strong physical reaction when receiving deliverance. Therefore, do not be disappointed if you do not receive in this manner. What you should expect is a release. You know there is a release when...

1. Oppressive force disappears;

2. Heaviness lifts;

3. Uneasiness goes away;

4. Burden or load lightens;

5. There is an inner sense of liberty, freedom, and divine satisfaction or contentment.

6. The joy of the Lord comes and you are able to rejoice!

The result of deliverance is –"righteousness, peace, and joy in the Holy Ghost"

Romans 14:17

"When devils are cast out, the Kingdom of God has come unto you."

Matthew 12:28

Demonic Manifestations

When evil spirits depart, you can normally expect to see some sort of manifestation through the mouth or nose. Listed below are some of the common manifestations;

- Coughing
- Drooling
- Vomiting
- Spitting
- Foaming
- Crying
- Screaming
- Sighing
- Roaring
- Belching
- Yawning
- Exhaling

Again, when demons are cast out, they normally leave through the mouth or the nose. Spirits are associated with breathing. Both the Hebrews and Greeks had only one word for spirit and breath. In the Greek, that word is *pneuma*. The Holy Spirit is breathed in (John 20:22). Evil spirits are breathed out. Sometimes people shake or tremble when they receive deliverance. Their body, in whole or part, may actually shake or tremble.

Hindrances to Receiving Deliverance
- Curses
- Sin
- Pride
- Passivity
- Ungodly Soul Ties
- Occultism
- Fear
- Embarrassment
- Unbelief
- Lack of Desire
- Unforgiveness
- Lack of Knowledge

All demons have legal and biblical grounds to occupy a person. They may not torment at will. If demons have legal grounds, then they have the right to remain. These legal grounds must be destroyed, in order to receive and maintain deliverance.

How To Keep Your Deliverance
- Read God's Word daily.

- Find a group of Bible-believing people, preferably a church, and regularly meet with them for worship, study, and ministry.

- Pray with the understanding and in tongues.

- Apply the blood of Jesus upon yourself and your family.

- Determine as nearly as you can which specific spirits have been cast out of you. Make a list of these areas because Satan will try to recapture them.

- The way demons gain re-entry is through a lax, undisciplined thought life. The mind is the battlefield. You must cast down imaginations and bring every thought into the obedience of Christ (II Corinthians 10:5).

- Pray to the Father fervently, asking Him to make you alert, sober, and vigilant against wrong thoughts (I Peter 5:8-9).

- The demons signal their approach to you by the fact that the old thought patterns you once had are now trying to return unto you. When this happens, immediately rebuke them. Declare verbally that you refuse them as quickly as possible.

- You have the authority to loose the angels of the Lord to battle demons (Hebrews 1:14; Matthew 18:18).

- Bind the demons and loose upon them the spirits of destruction (I Chronicles 21:12) and burning and judgment (Isaiah 4:4) from the Lord Jesus Christ.

- Also loose warrior angels upon the demons.

Ephesians 4:26-27 charges believers, "Be ye angry, and sin not: let not the sun go down upon your wrath: Neither give place to the devil." The devil is a legalist and is very much aware of his rights. Anger; specially unresolved, will definitely give the devil a place in our lives. He cannot be everywhere at the same time. However, he will send his demons to harass and torment those who yield to him.

RELATED SPIRITS OF ANGER, WRATH, AND MALICE

Agitation	Hardness
Anxiety	Harshness
Animosity	Hatred
Anti-submissiveness	Haughtiness
Argument	Hostility
Anxiety	Hurt
Blasphemy	Impatience
Boasting	Intolerance
Bickering	Insanity
Bitterness	Insecurity
Combative	Jealousy
Conspiracy	Loneliness
Contention	Lust
Cruelty	Lunacy
Cursing	Lying
Dominance	Madness
Defensive	Malevolence
Defiance	Malicious
Destruction	Mania
Ego	Murder
Envy	Prejudice
Fighting	Pride
Frustration	Rage
Fury	Rebellion
Gall	Rejection

Resentment
Retaliation
Revenge
Ruthless
Selfishness
Self-Centered
Self-Hatred
Spite
Strife
Stubbornness
Temper
Turmoil
Unapologetic
Unforgiveness
Violence
Witchcraft
Wrath

PRAYER OF REPENTANCE AND RENUNCIATION OF SPIRITS OF ANGER, WRATH, AND MALICE

Heavenly Father,

I come to you now in the name of your precious son Jesus Christ who died on the cross for my sin. I now confess that anger no longer has control over my life. I cut all bands, links, ties and cords that have linked my family and me to the works of the spirit of anger. Ephesians 4:31 proclaims, "let all bitterness, wrath, anger, clamour and evil speaking be put away from me with all malice." I choose to forgive those that have hurt or disappointed me and release them and myself from all spirits of anger by embracing and releasing your eternal love.

In Jesus Name Amen!

.

More Great Resources From
Stephen A. Garner Ministries

Books

- Apostolic Pioneering
- Benefits of Praying in Tongues
- Essentials of the Prophetic Ministry
- Fundamentals of Deliverance 101, Revised and Expanded
- Pray Without Ceasing Special Edition
- Ministering Spirits: "Engaging the Angelic Realm"
- Deliver Us From Evil
- Kingdom Prayer
- Restoring Prophetic Watchmen
- The Kingdom of God: A Believer's Guide to Kingdom Living
- Prayers, Decrees and Confessions for Wisdom
- Prayers, Decrees and Confessions for Favour & Grace
- Prayers, Decrees and Confessions for Prosperity
- Prayers, Decrees and Confessions for Increase
- Prayers, Decrees and Confessions for Power
- Prayers, Decrees and Confessions for Goodness and Mercy
- Prayers that Strengthen Marriages and Families
- Prayers, Decrees and Confessions for Righteousness, Revised & Expanded

CD's

- Prayers For The Nations
- Prayers Against Python & Witchcraft
- Prayers Of Healing & Restoration
- Prayers of Renunciation and Deliverance
- Thy Kingdom Come
- Latter Rain
- The Glory
- Overcoming Spirits of Terrorism
- Songs of Intercession
- The Spirit of the Breaker
- The Fear of the Lord

CONTACT INFORMATION
STEPHEN A. GARNER MINISTRIES
P.O. BOX 1545, BOLINGBROOK, IL 60440
EMAIL: SAGARNERMINISTRIES@GMAIL.COM
WWW.SAGMINISTRIES.COM